D1682303

THE BOY WHO HARNESSED THE WIND

William Kamkwamba and Bryan Mealer

pictures by Elizabeth Zunon

DIAL BOOKS FOR YOUNG READERS
an imprint of Penguin Group (USA) Inc.

In a small village in Malawi, where people had no money for lights, nightfall came quickly and hurried poor farmers to bed.
But for William, the darkness was best for dreaming.

He dreamed of building things and taking them apart,
like the trucks with bottle-cap wheels parked under his bed
and pieces of radios that he'd crack open and wonder,
If I can hear the music, then where is the band?

His grandpa's tales of magic also whispered in the pitch-black of his room. Witch planes passed through the window while ghost dancers twirled around the room, as if a hundred men were inside their bodies.

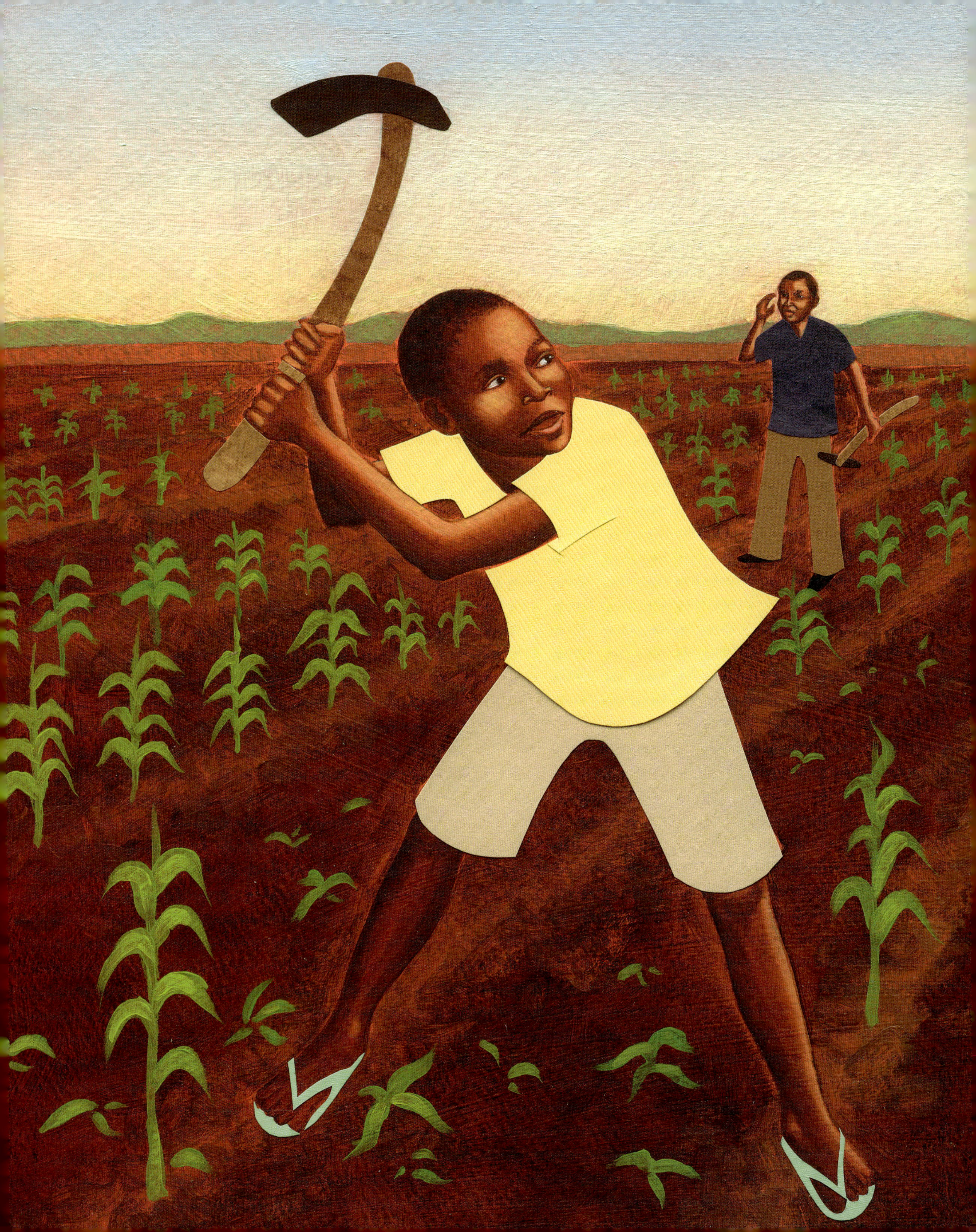

At dawn in the fields,

William scanned the maize rows for magical beings,

then wondered as a truck rumbled past,

How does its engine make it go?

"Pay attention where you throw that hoe!" his father shouted.

"You'll cut off your foot."

For all its power over dancers and flying things,
magic could not bring the rain.
Without water, the sun rose angry each morning and
scorched the fields, turning the maize into dust.
Without food, Malawi began to starve.

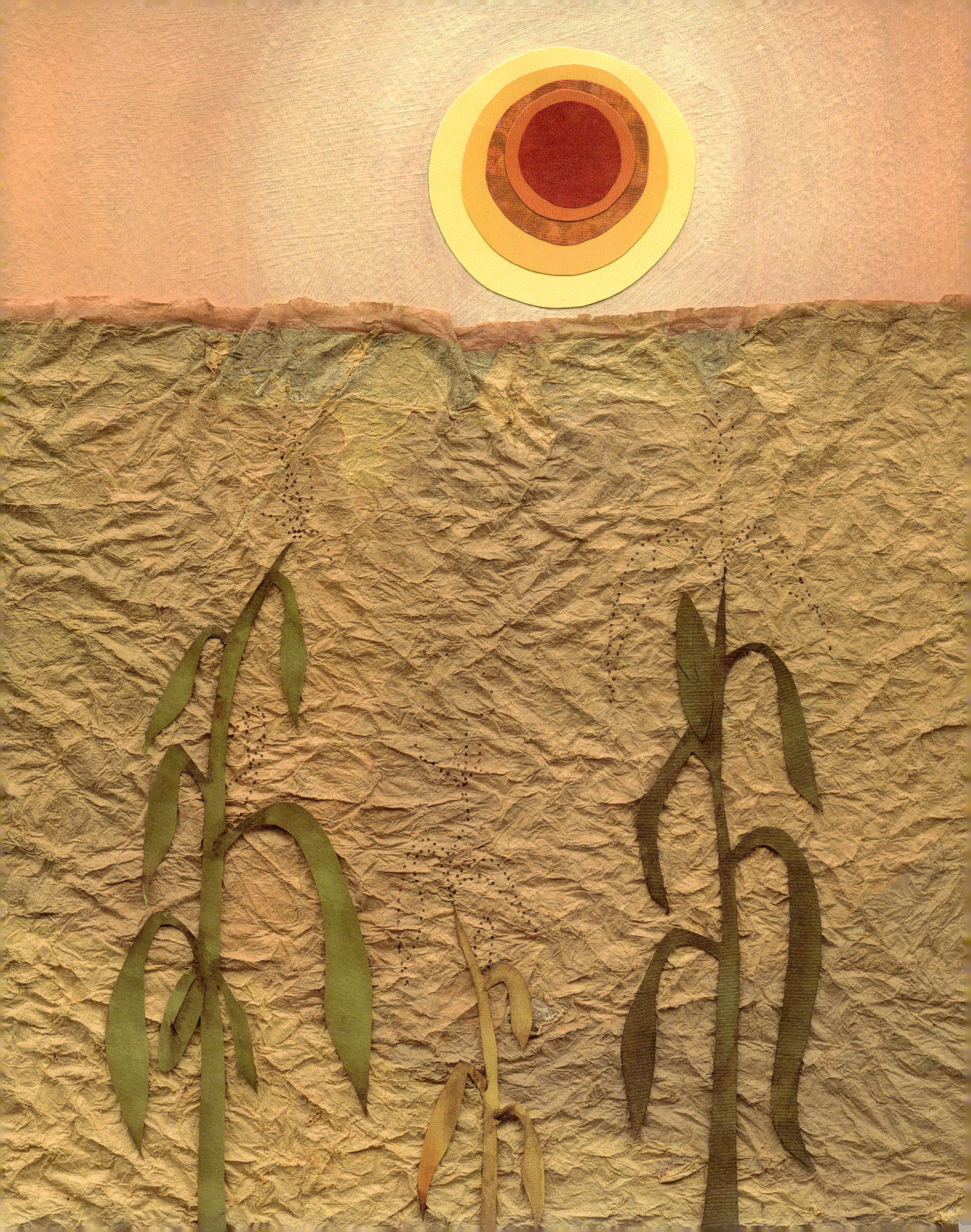

Soon William's father gathered the children and said,
"From now on, we eat only one meal per day. Make it last."
In the evenings, they sat around the lantern and ate their handful,
watching hungry people pass like spirits along the roads.

Money also disappeared with the rain.
"Pepani," his father said. "I am sorry. You will have to drop out of school."
Now William stood on the road and watched the lucky students pass,
alone with the monster in his belly and the lump in his throat.
For weeks he sulked under the mango tree,
until he remembered the library down the road,
a gift from the Americans.

He found science books filled with brilliant pictures.
With his English dictionary close by, William put together
how engines moved those big trucks,
and how radios pulled their music from the sky.
But the greatest picture of all was a machine
taller than the tallest tree with blades like a fan.

A giant pinwheel?
Something to catch magic?

Slowly, he built the sentence:
"Windmills can produce electricity and pump water."

He closed his eyes and saw
a windmill outside his home,
pulling electricity from the breeze
and bringing light to the dark valley.

He saw the machine drawing cool water from the ground,
sending it gushing through the thirsty fields,
turning the maize tall and green,
even when farmers' prayers for rain went unanswered.
This windmill was more than a machine.
It was a weapon to fight hunger.

"*Magesti a mphepo,*" he whispered:

I will build electric wind.

In the junk yard, pieces appeared
like rusted treasures in the tall grass.
A tractor fan. Some pipe.
And bearings and bolts that required every muscle to remove.

"*Tonga!*" he'd shout to the birds and spiders,
holding up his prize.
But as William dragged his metals home,
people called out,
"This boy is *misala*. Only crazy people play with trash!"

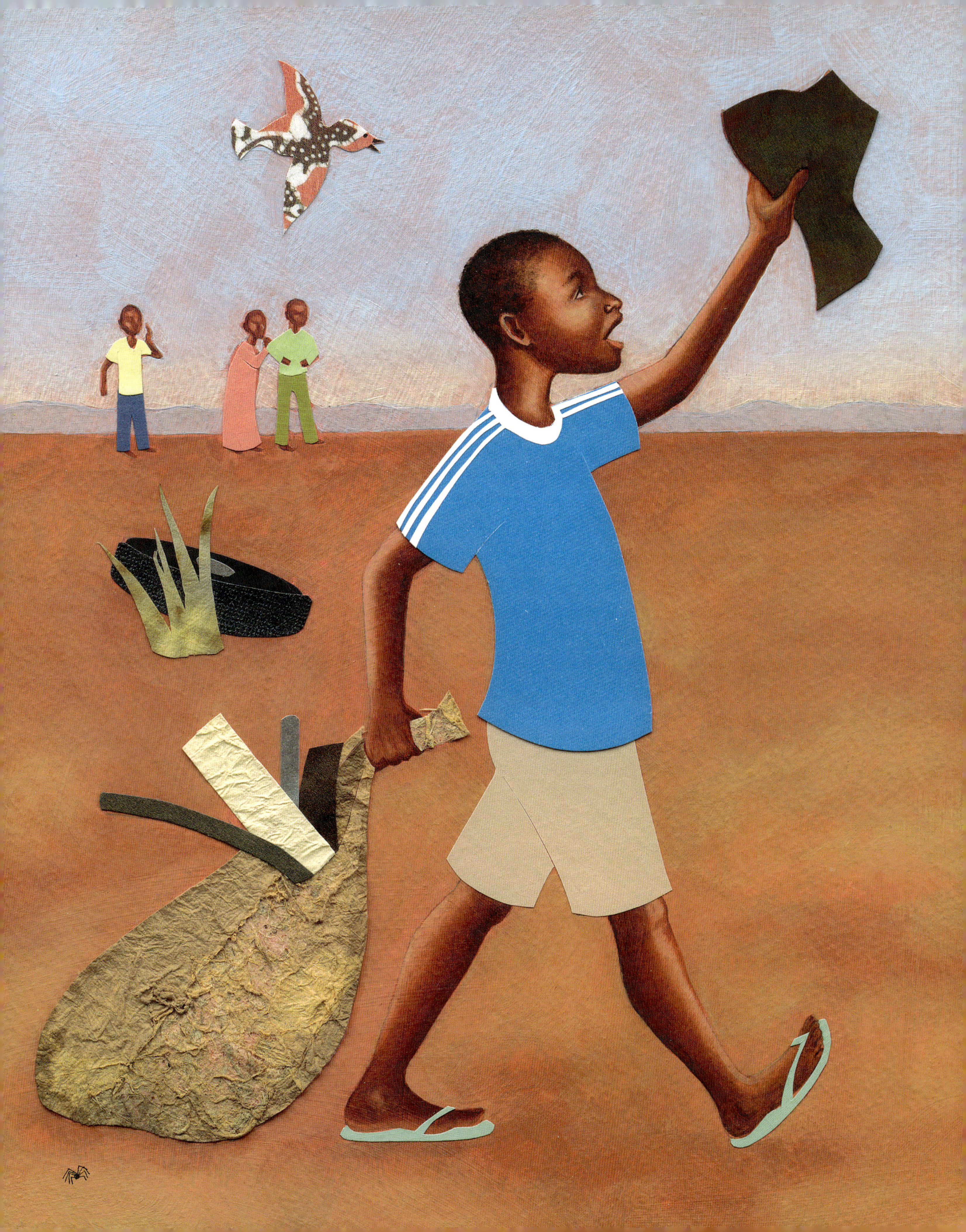

After many weeks, William arranged his pieces in the dirt:
a broken bicycle, rusted bottle caps, and plastic pipe,
even a small generator that powered a headlight on a bike.

For three days, he bolted, banged, and tinkered while chickens squawked and dogs barked and neighbors shook their heads, saying, "What's *misala* doing now?"

His cousin Geoffrey and best friend Gilbert soon appeared.
"Muli bwanji," they greeted. "Can we help with electric wind?"
"Grab your pangas and follow me," he said, and took them into the forest.
Together, they swung their sharp blades into the trunks of blue gum trees,
then hammered them together to make the tower.

Standing atop, William shouted,

"Bring it up!"

while the boys tugged and heaved.

A crowd gathered below and gazed at this strange machine

that now leaned and wobbled like a clumsy giraffe.

Some giggled, others teased, but William waited for the wind.

Like always, it came,

first a breeze, then a gusting gale.

The tower swayed and the blades spun round.

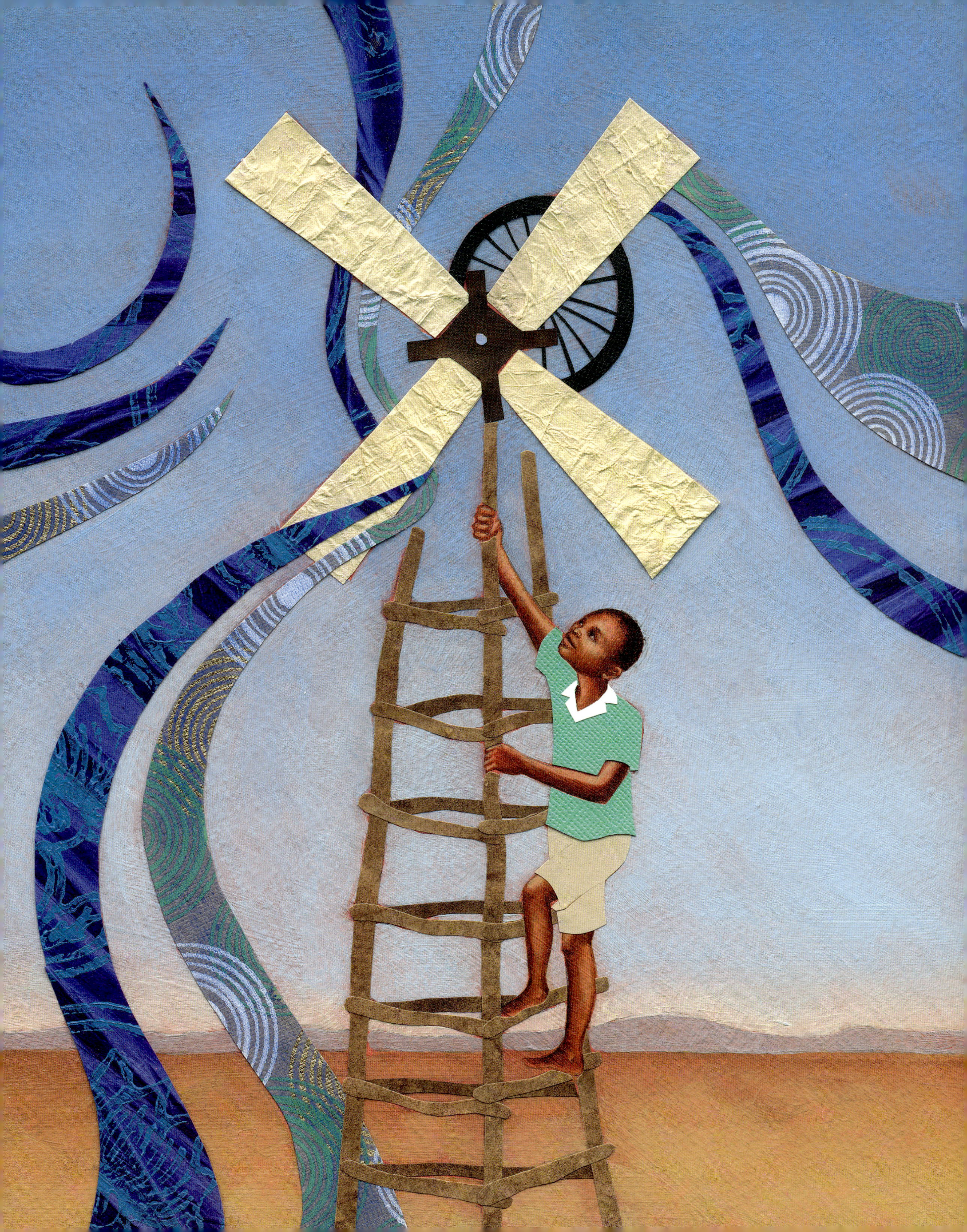

With sore hands once slowed by hunger and darkness
William connected wires to a small bulb, which flickered at first,
then surged as bright as the sun.

"Tonga!" he shouted. "I have made electric wind!"

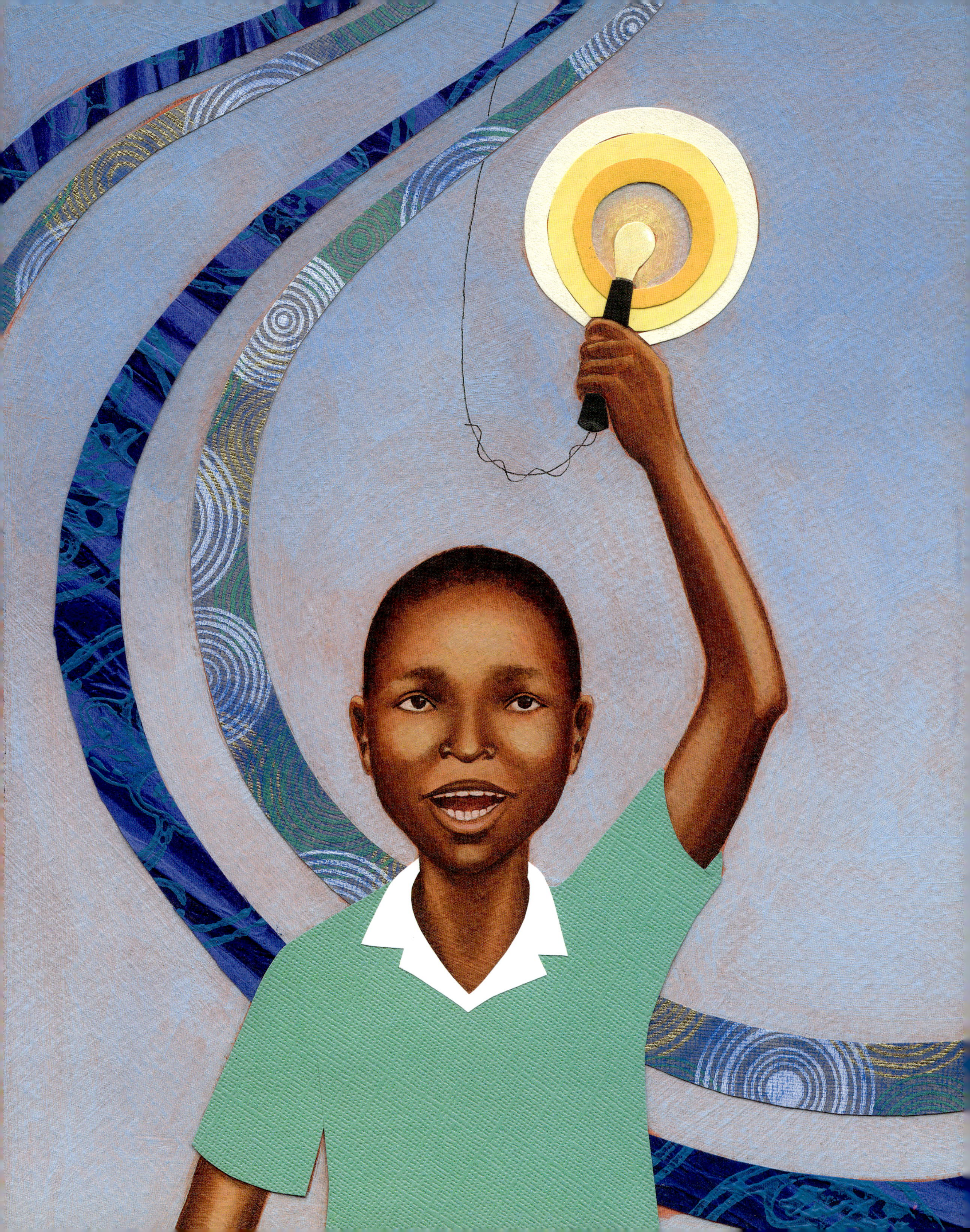

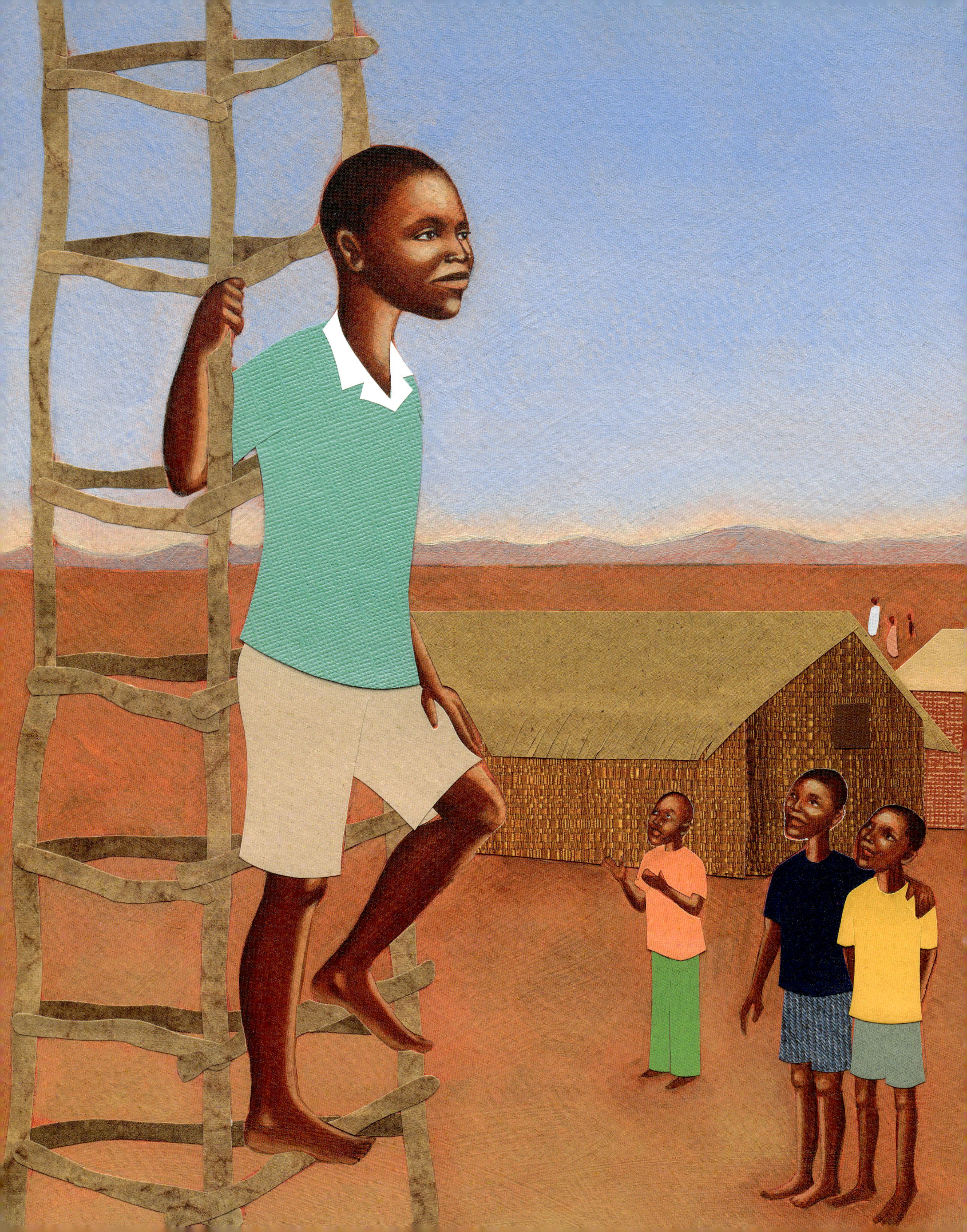

"*Wachitabwina!*" a man yelled. "Well done!"
As the doubters clapped and cheered,
William knew he had just begun.
Light could not fill empty bellies,
but another windmill could soak the dry ground,
creating food where once there was none.
Magesti a mphepo—electric wind—can feed my country, William thought.

And that was the strongest magic of all.

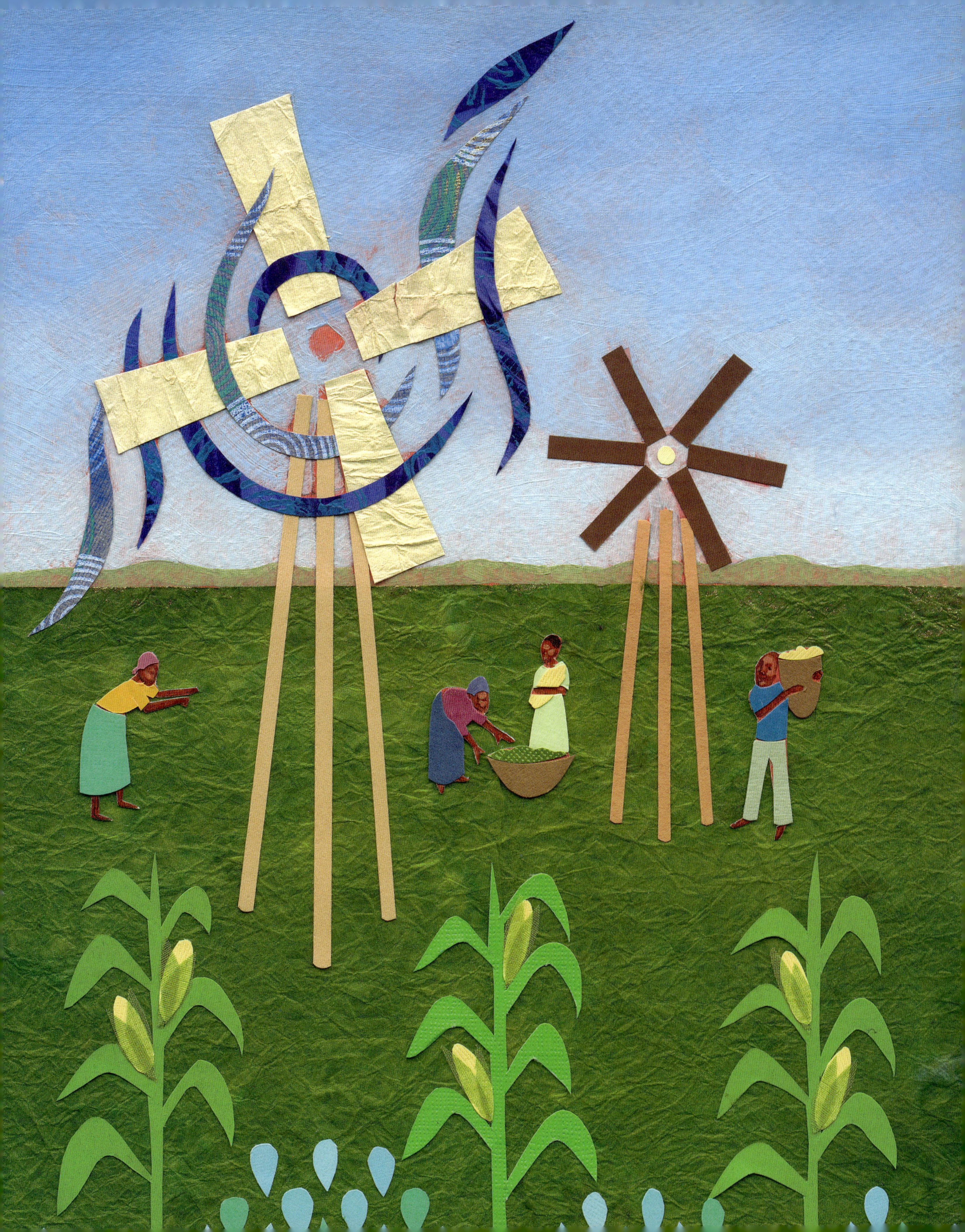

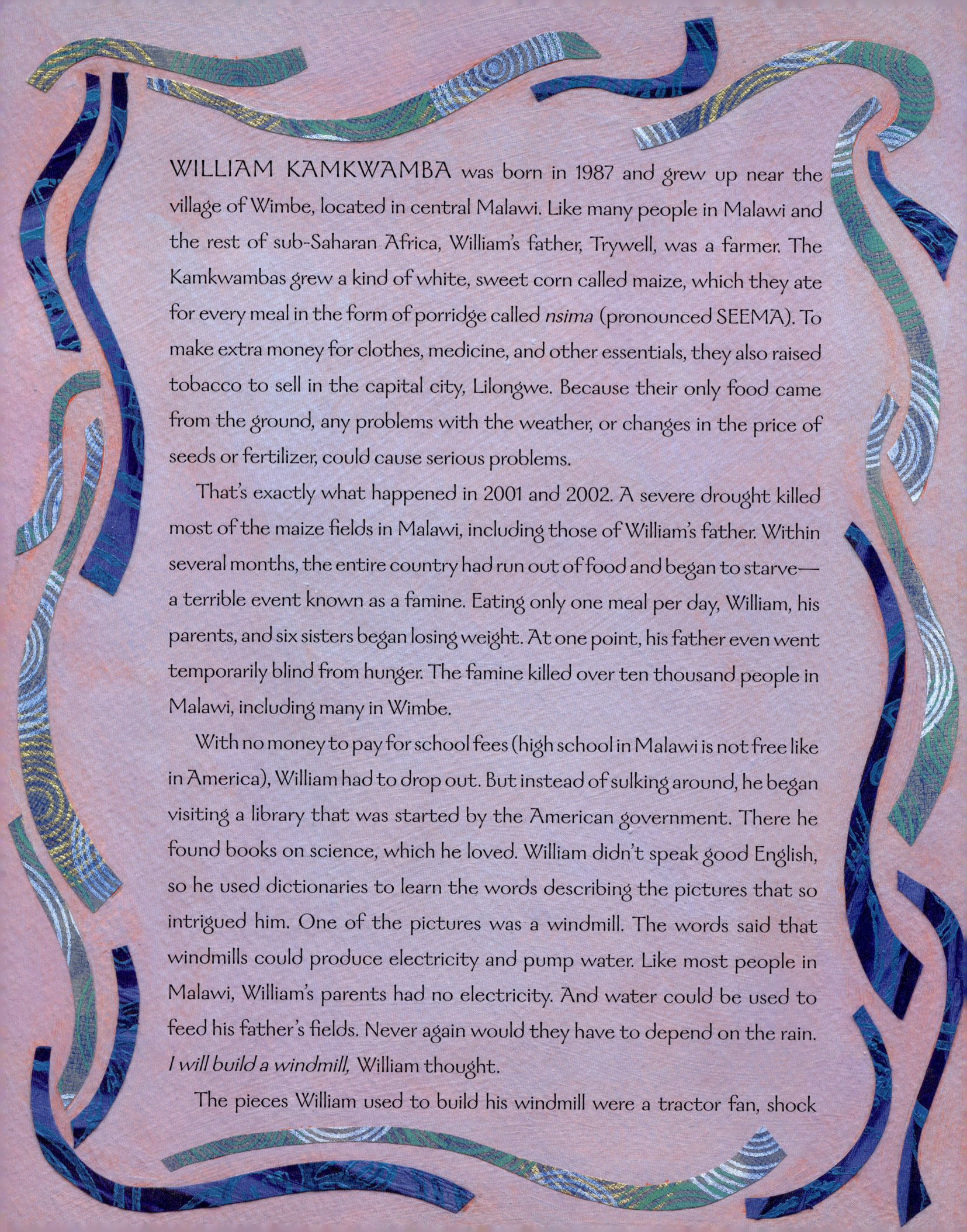

WILLIAM KAMKWAMBA was born in 1987 and grew up near the village of Wimbe, located in central Malawi. Like many people in Malawi and the rest of sub-Saharan Africa, William's father, Trywell, was a farmer. The Kamkwambas grew a kind of white, sweet corn called maize, which they ate for every meal in the form of porridge called *nsima* (pronounced SEEMA). To make extra money for clothes, medicine, and other essentials, they also raised tobacco to sell in the capital city, Lilongwe. Because their only food came from the ground, any problems with the weather, or changes in the price of seeds or fertilizer, could cause serious problems.

That's exactly what happened in 2001 and 2002. A severe drought killed most of the maize fields in Malawi, including those of William's father. Within several months, the entire country had run out of food and began to starve—a terrible event known as a famine. Eating only one meal per day, William, his parents, and six sisters began losing weight. At one point, his father even went temporarily blind from hunger. The famine killed over ten thousand people in Malawi, including many in Wimbe.

With no money to pay for school fees (high school in Malawi is not free like in America), William had to drop out. But instead of sulking around, he began visiting a library that was started by the American government. There he found books on science, which he loved. William didn't speak good English, so he used dictionaries to learn the words describing the pictures that so intrigued him. One of the pictures was a windmill. The words said that windmills could produce electricity and pump water. Like most people in Malawi, William's parents had no electricity. And water could be used to feed his father's fields. Never again would they have to depend on the rain. *I will build a windmill,* William thought.

The pieces William used to build his windmill were a tractor fan, shock absorber, and the frame of a broken bicycle missing a wheel. For blades, he melted plastic pipe over a fire and flattened them, then carved their shape with a saw. For a generator, he used a dynamo, which is a tiny bottle-shaped device that produces electricity by turning magnets inside a coil of wire, something called electromagnetism. When the wind blew, the blades acted like pedals and spun the tire, which turned the coils inside the dynamo and produced a current. A wire from the dynamo reached down to William's room and powered a small lightbulb. He was fourteen years old.

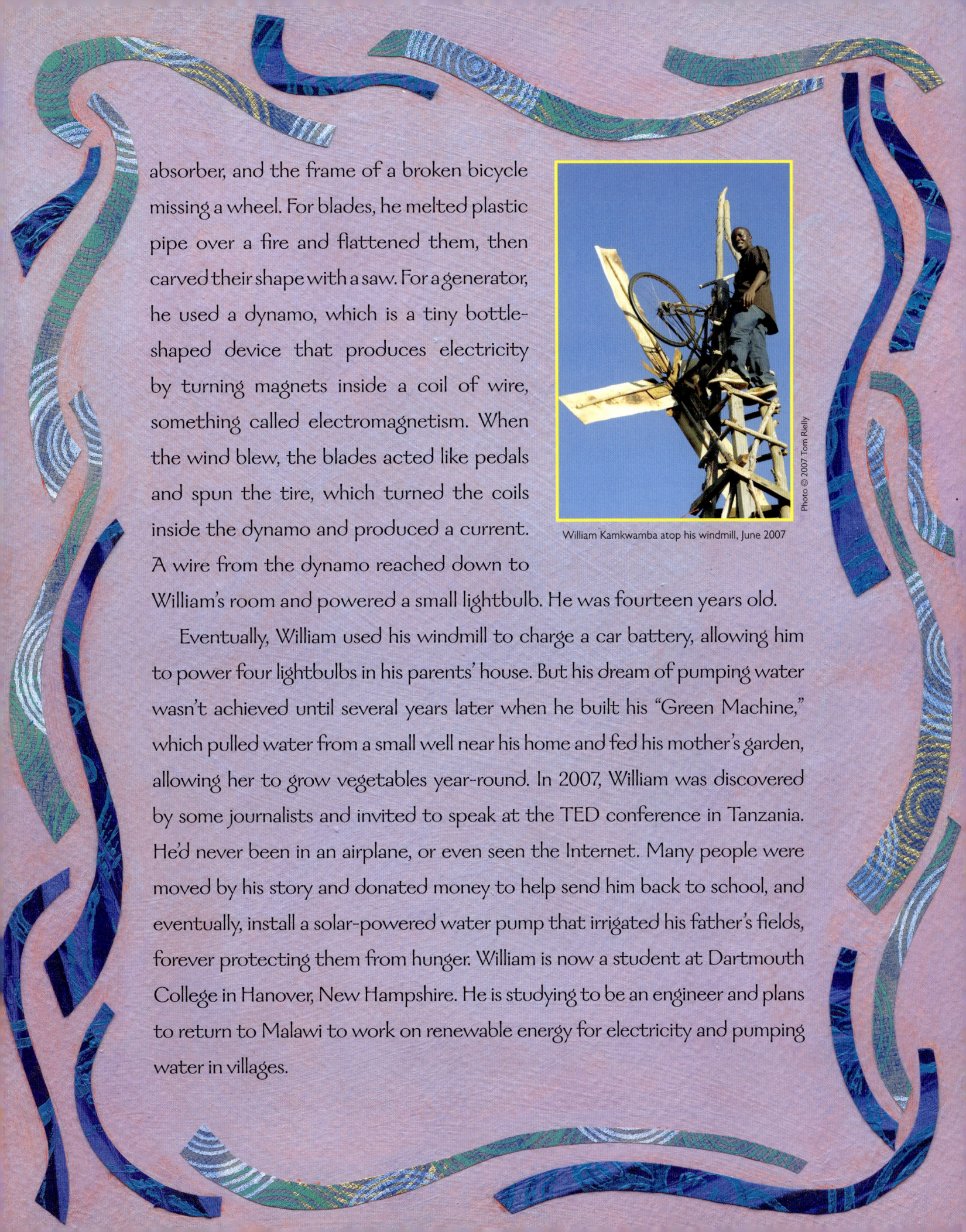

William Kamkwamba atop his windmill, June 2007

Eventually, William used his windmill to charge a car battery, allowing him to power four lightbulbs in his parents' house. But his dream of pumping water wasn't achieved until several years later when he built his "Green Machine," which pulled water from a small well near his home and fed his mother's garden, allowing her to grow vegetables year-round. In 2007, William was discovered by some journalists and invited to speak at the TED conference in Tanzania. He'd never been in an airplane, or even seen the Internet. Many people were moved by his story and donated money to help send him back to school, and eventually, install a solar-powered water pump that irrigated his father's fields, forever protecting them from hunger. William is now a student at Dartmouth College in Hanover, New Hampshire. He is studying to be an engineer and plans to return to Malawi to work on renewable energy for electricity and pumping water in villages.

For Tiyamike
—W. K.

For Nolan
—B.M.

For Justin Yuen, whose strength, courage, passion and spirit will always inspire those who knew him.
—E.Z.

DIAL BOOKS FOR YOUNG READERS
A division of Penguin Young Readers Group
Published by The Penguin Group
Penguin Group (USA) Inc., 375 Hudson Street, New York, NY 10014, U.S.A.
Penguin Group (Canada), 90 Eglinton Avenue East, Suite 700, Toronto, Ontario, Canada M4P 2Y3 (a division of Pearson Penguin Canada Inc.)
Penguin Books Ltd, 80 Strand, London WC2R 0RL, England
Penguin Ireland, 25 St. Stephen's Green, Dublin 2, Ireland (a division of Penguin Books Ltd)
Penguin Group (Australia), 250 Camberwell Road, Camberwell, Victoria 3124, Australia (a division of Pearson Australia Group Pty Ltd)
Penguin Books India Pvt Ltd, 11 Community Centre, Panchsheel Park, New Delhi - 110 017, India
Penguin Group (NZ), 67 Apollo Drive, Rosedale, Auckland 0632, New Zealand (a division of Pearson New Zealand Ltd)
Penguin Books (South Africa) (Pty) Ltd, 24 Sturdee Avenue, Rosebank, Johannesburg 2196, South Africa
Penguin Books Ltd, Registered Offices: 80 Strand, London WC2R 0RL, England

Text copyright © 2012 by William Kamkwamba and Bryan Mealer
Illustrations copyright © 2012 by Elizabeth Zunon
All rights reserved
The publisher does not have any control over and does not assume any responsibility for author or third-party websites or their content.

Designed by Jasmin Rubero
Text set in Galahad Std
Manufactured in China on acid-free paper

1 3 5 7 9 10 8 6 4 2

Library of Congress Cataloging-in-Publication Data
Kamkwamba, William, date.
The boy who harnessed the wind / by William Kamkwamba and Bryan Mealer ; pictures by Elizabeth Zunon.
p. cm.
Summary: The story of William Kamkwamba, who in 2001 at the age of fourteen taught himself to build a windmill and bring electricity to his Malawi village during a period of drought and famine.
ISBN 978-0-8037-3511-8 (hardback : acid-free paper)
1. Kamkwamba, William, date—Juvenile literature. 2. Mechanical engineers—Malawi—Biography—Juvenile literature. 3. Windmills—Malawi—Juvenile literature. 4. Electric power production—Malawi—Juvenile literature. 5. Irrigation—Malawi—Juvenile literature. I. Mealer, Bryan. II. Zunon, Elizabeth, ill. III. Title.
TJ140.K36A3 2012   621.4'53096897—dc23   2011021536

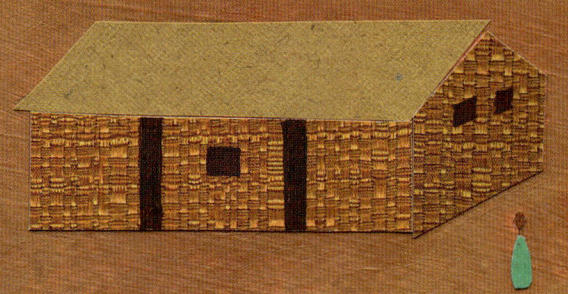

The art was created using oil paint and cut paper.

Read a book. Give a book.
Combining the joy of reading with the power of helping others.
WEGIVEBOOKS.ORG

FEB 1 5 2012